A New True Book

PREDATORS

By Mark Rosenthal

This "true book" was prepared
under the direction of
Illa Podendorf,
formerly with the Laboratory School,
University of Chicago

CHILDRENS PRESS, CHICAGO

Young great horned owl
eating a chipmunk.

PHOTO CREDITS

Allan Roberts—Cover, 2, 9 (top), 11, 13 (right), 15
(2 photos), 16, 21 (2 photos, bottom), 22 (top), 25
(2 photos), 28 (right), 33 (2 photos), 35, 38, 45 (left)

Lynn M. Stone—4, 9 (bottom left), 12, 14, 17
(2 photos), 22 (bottom), 24 (right), 27 (left), 34 (left),
37 (right), 43 (right), 45 (right)

Mark A. Rosenthal—6, 18 (3 photos), 21 (top), 27
(right), 29, 31 (top), 40

James P. Rowan—7, 37 (top & bottom left), 43 (left)

Jerry Hennen—8, 9 (bottom right), 13 (left), 28 (left),
34 (right)

Reinhard Brucker—24 (left)

Miami Seaquarium—31 (bottom)

COVER—Great horned owl and pilot blacksnake

Library of Congress Cataloging in Publication Data

Rosenthal, Mark.
    Predators.

    (A New true book)
    Includes index.
    Summary: Describes briefly the characteristics and
natural environment of various predatory animals and
discusses some of their problems in finding food.
    1. Predatory animals—Juvenile literature.
[1. Predatory animals] I. Title. II. Series.
QL758.R67   1983   596'.053   83-7512
ISBN 0-516-01707-1   AACR2

TABLE OF CONTENTS

Male African lion. All lions eat meat.

WHAT IS A PREDATOR?

A predator is any animal that kills and eats another animal. A predator uses the flesh of the animal it kills as food to live.

Some animals eat plants and grass as their main foods. The digestive system of the lion will not let it eat plant material as an everyday diet. The lion

Female lion. Lions hunt zebras and other animals.

is a carnivore, or meat-
eating, animal. It hunts
other animals as food. The
lion is a predator.

All animals need to eat
food to live. A predator
can be a mammal, bird,
reptile, or even an insect.

Polar bear

WHERE PREDATORS LIVE

Predators can be found everywhere.

In Arctic regions the polar bear hunts for seals. The lion and leopard hunt antelope that graze the open plains of Africa. The

Masked shrew

forest of evergreens is home for members of the weasel family.

Rodents are the main prey of snakes that live in desert regions.

Predators can be found in the forests. Under the leaf litter of the forest floor are small shrews that hunt and eat earthworms.

The adult least weasel (above), grows to be only eight inches long. The bullsnake (below left) and the golden mantled ground squirrel (below right) are meat-eating predators.

HOW PREDATORS
CATCH THEIR FOOD

Most predators hunt for the food they eat. The animal that a predator hunts and eats is called the prey.

Some predators such as the lion, tiger, or cheetah can outrun their prey over a short distance. Over a long distance, the prey animal has the advantage. This means

Tiger ready to attack

predators must first get close
to their prey. They move
quietly. They keep low and
close to the ground and use
vegetation to hide behind.
This is called stalking.

11

Wolves hunt bison in packs.

When they are very close
to the animal, they leap out
and charge the prey.
Sometimes they catch it, but
many times they fail.

Some animals do not stalk
their food. Instead, they count
on a disguise to fool the prey.

The snapping turtle (left) and the praying mantis, eating a cricket, (above) stay very still. When their prey comes near, they attack.

The alligator snapping turtle will lie on the bottom of a pond and open its mouth to wiggle its pink tongue. The tongue looks like a worm. When fish come close to see what is wiggling, the turtle can quickly reach out and grab its dinner.

Timber wolves. When a wolf pack hunts, each animal has a special job to do.

Many predators hunt alone, but some hunt in groups. Killer whales, porpoises, and wolves all hunt in groups. When a prey animal is sighted, the hunting pack fans out and tries to encircle the prey.

The killer whale (left) and the
porpoise (above) hunt in groups.

Animals that hunt in
groups must be able to
work together to be
successful.

Most predators will hunt
only when they are hungry.
A mother with babies has

Female mountain lion or puma and her three-week-old babies. The cubs must learn to hunt in order to survive.

to hunt for their food. As the young grow older, the mother teaches them to hunt for themselves. It may take many years and much practice to become a good hunter.

16

The bull frog (left) and tiger salamander (right) are excellent hunters.

FOOD OF THE PREDATOR

Land animals hunted by predators have to be very alert. They must have good hearing, good eyesight, and a good sense of smell. A strange smell or a sudden noise will alert them. They will freeze in place looking for danger.

Some animals protect themselves with speed and the ability to outrun a predator. The zebra and antelope of Africa live in herds for protection. If one

Zebras (above left), Thompson's gazelles (left) and musk ox (above) live in herds for protection.

animal has its head down
feeding, others will be
watching for hunters.

When wolves approach a
musk ox herd, the herd
moves into a circle with
the youngsters protected in
the middle. The adults face
outward with their horns as
weapons against the
predators. This is a very
good defense against
predators that hunt in
groups.

91-13594

Some animals have weapons called antlers. These can be used as a defensive weapon against hunters.

The oddest protection against predators is found on the porcupine. It has developed special hair called quills. The quills are very sharp. Any animal that tries to grab a porcupine will wind up with its mouth and paws full of sharp, painful quills.

The porcupine (above) uses its quills for protection. The bull moose (below left) and the male elk can use their antlers.

The coyote is a member of the wolf family.

Bengal tigers live in jungle forests.

PREDATORS
OF THE LAND

Predators that live on the land come in all sizes and shapes.

The tiger hunts during the early evening. It hunts deer, wild pigs, or sometimes the cattle of native tribesmen.

Smaller hunters can be found living on the prairies of North America. The coyote hunts prairie dogs.

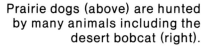
Prairie dogs (above) are hunted by many animals including the desert bobcat (right).

These little rodents are food not only for the coyotes but also for hungry bobcats and ferrets.

Some land predators will travel into trees in search of food.

A kingsnake (above) swallows
a live garter snake. A common
water snake (left) swallows
a minnow.

The king cobra, a large
poisonous snake, eats only
other snakes. Some snakes
and lizards catch smaller
frogs, fish, and amphibians
as a main part of their
diets.

PREDATORS OF THE AIR

Hunters that fly can be very dangerous.

Birds of prey, such as owls, falcons, eagles, and hawks, are true predators. They spend their days or evenings searching for food.

Some birds are also good fishermen. An eagle can swoop down and grab a big fish right out of

The great horned owl (left) and the harpy eagle (right)
fly silently and swoop down on their prey.

shallow water. The giant
harpy eagle from South
America hunts in the forest.
It has very keen eyesight.

Some animals that fly
use a special tool called
echo location instead of
eyesight.

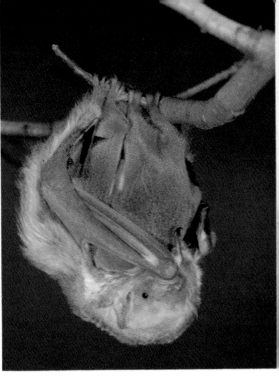

Brown bat (above) and a female
red bat with three babies (right).
Bats are the only true flying mammals.

The bat gives out high-
pitched sounds that
bounce off the insects and
come back to the bat.
These sounds tell the bat
how far away the insects
are and in what direction
they are flying.

California sea lions

PREDATORS
OF THE WATER

Even in the water there are predator animals.

The killer whale hunts in packs for seals, penguins, and sometimes even other whales.

Seals and sea lions are hunters of fish.

They have sharp teeth to catch and hold their prey.

The crocodile is a hunter that will eat anything it can grab.

The shark is one of the largest predators of the sea. It is an excellent swimmer. The great white shark can grow to more than twenty feet long.

Nile crocodile (above) and the shark (below)

TOOLS OF
THE PREDATORS

Hunting animals need special tools to catch and hold their prey.

All cats, except for the cheetah, have claws that they can pull in or push out. When cats grab an animal, they use their claws.

A house cat (above) and bobcat (below) use their claws to catch their prey, but they kill with their sharp teeth.

Red-tailed hawk (left) and hawk talons (right)

Birds of prey have sharp beaks for ripping and tearing food. They use their talons to grip their prey and kill it.

The chameleon captures its prey with its long sticky tongue. It needs good

The chameleon hunts with its sticky tongue.

eyesight to judge the distance between itself and its prey. When it thinks the distance is correct, it sticks its tongue out in a quick flash and grabs an insect.

Predators must have good eyesight to help locate their prey.

Animals like the anteater from Central and South America and the echidna from Australia use powerful digging claws to rip apart ant and termite mounds. They use their long sticky tongues to eat the insects.

Sometimes predators depend on an excellent sense of hearing. The barn owl can catch a mouse in complete darkness just by

Giant anteater (top left),
cheetahs (left),
and barn owl (above)

using its sense of hearing
to locate the animal.

Speed is important to
predators. When a cheetah
chases a gazelle, it must
use great speed to get
close to the animal.

37

A red fox trys to eat a box turtle. Although the turtle may lose some toes to this predator, when its shell is tightly closed, the fox will not be able to kill it.

PREDATORS
HAVE PROBLEMS

Predators are not always successful when they hunt. Many times they come back without any meal. A coyote may find it hard to sneak up on prairie dogs. If the prairie dogs see a predator, they give an alarm. This lets all the animals know that danger is near. All the prairie dogs then dive into the safety of their tunnels.

Sometimes a lion will charge, but the animal will be too far away. The lion will not be able to run a long distance to grab the prey. Another one gets away.

Many predators kill more than they can eat at one time. When this happens they must store the extra food. They must protect the food from scavengers that are always ready to steal food.

Lions, jackals, and hyenas, often scavenge food rather than hunt for themselves.

Striped hyenas are scavengers. They eat leftover food.

ENDANGERED PREDATORS

Certain predators have become endangered. Their numbers in the wild have become so low that scientists are not certain if they can survive and reproduce. They need laws to protect them.

In India the Gir Forest is a national forest. The only Asiatic lions in the world live here. There are only about two hundred lions left. Farmers live close to this area. Sometimes the lions will kill one of their cattle. It is sometimes difficult for people to live close to large predators.

The polar bear lives in the Arctic regions. It does not live close to people, but still needs laws to protect it.

The bald eagle is the national bird of the United

The Indian lion (left) and the bald eagle (above) need special laws to protect them.

States. It is a large bird of prey that once was common in North America. Now its numbers are low. Only in Alaska can the bald eagle be seen in great numbers. It is a protected predator.

THINGS TO REMEMBER

A predator is a meat-eating animal that needs food to live.

Predators can be found throughout the world. They come in all shapes and sizes. They live in the air, on land, and in the water.

Most predators hunt only when they are hungry. They have special claws, beaks, and senses to help them hunt and kill.

Gila monster (above), eating baby birds, and the robber fly (right), eating a butterfly, must hunt in order to live.

The way of life of predators is a normal part of the world of nature. We must help endangered predators to survive by protecting them with special laws.

WORDS YOU SHOULD KNOW

advantage(ad • VAN • tij) — to have a better chance; benefit
alarm(ah • LARM) — a sound or signal that warns
alert(ah • LERT) — watchful; on guard
antlers(ANT • lerz) — solid horns of an animal
carnivore(CAR • nih • vor) — a meat-eating animal
charge(CHARJ) — to rush to attack
digestive system(dih • JESS • tiv SIS • tum) — parts of the body
        that break down food so it can be used for
        energy
disguise(diss • GIZE) — to hide; to conceal
encircle(en • SIR • kil) — to form a circle around
endangered(en • DAIN • jerd) — threatened with danger
pack(PAK) — a group
predator(PRED • ah • ter) — an animal that kills and eats other
     animals
prey(PRAY) — an animal that is hunted and eaten by another
    animal
reproduce(re • pro • DOOCE) — to make new individuals of the
     same kind
stalking(STAWK • ing) — the act of hunting quietly with great care
survive(sir • VYVE) — to stay alive
talons(TAL • onz) — the claws of a bird of prey

INDEX

About the Author

Mark Rosenthal majored in Zoology at Southern Illinois University in Carbondale, Illinois. He received his Masters of Arts degree in Zoology from Northeastern Illinois State University in Chicago, Illinois. He is presently the Curator of Mammals at the Lincoln Park Zoological Gardens in Chicago.

Mark has contributed to many scientific publications including the International Zoo Yearbook, The American Association of Zoological Parks and Aquariums, The Ark *(Lincoln Park Zoological Society),* Primates, *and* The Animal Keepers Forum. *The New True Book of Bears is his first publication directed to young readers. Many of Mark's photographs have appeared in other volumes in the True Book series.*